CALLED OUT

A BLUEPRINT
FOR WALKING IN YOUR CALLING
WITH CLARITY, CONFIDENCE, AND COURAGE

KRISTA PETTIFORD

MAKK Publishing Co

SAN DIEGO, CALIFORNIA

Copyright © 2019 Krista Pettiford

MAKK Publishing Co.
ISBN: 978-0-9823805-8-1
Library of Congress Control Number: 2019908665

All rights reserved. No part of this publication may be reproduced, distributed or transmitted in any form or by any means, including photocopying, recording, or other electronic or mechanical methods, without the prior written permission of the publisher, except in the case of brief quotations embodied in critical reviews and certain other noncommercial uses permitted by copyright law.

For permission requests, write to the publisher, addressed "Attention: Permissions Coordinator," at the address below.

Unless otherwise indicated Scripture quotations are from New King James Version®. Copyright © 1982 by Thomas Nelson, Inc. Used by permission. All rights reserved.

Scripture quotations taken from the Amplified® Bible (AMPC),
Copyright © 1954, 1958, 1962, 1964, 1965, 1987 by The Lockman Foundation Used by permission.

Scripture is taken from GOD'S WORD®, © 1995 God's Word to the Nations. Used by permission of God's Word Mission Society.

This publication is not intended to provide professional advice. It is sold with the understanding that neither the author nor the publisher is engaged in rendering health, medical, or other professional services.

MAKK Publishing Co.
772 Jamacha Rd, El Cajon CA, 92019

Other books by Krista Pettiford

A Call to God's Daughters to Step into His L.A.B.

Surrendered Balance Daily Living for the Modern Christian Woman

*Prophetic Expressions
A Guide to Understanding Christ in the Biblical Calendar*

CONTENT

Introduction 7
Called Out 17
The Heart of the Father 22
   God's L.A.B. 24
   Your Spiritual Blessings and Inheritance 31
Handpicked 35
   Your Spiritual Gifts 41
Called to Be Authentic 47
Your Purpose and Your Mission 53
Your God-given Dreams and Visions 63
   Write Your Vision 67
Craft Your Motto 71
   Write Your Motto 74
Craft Your Calling Statement 76
   Write Your Calling Statement: 79
Reject False Mindsets 81
   Replace Lies With Truth 86
Say What God Says About You 89

Take Courage 97
The Long Run 104
Upward 109
Choose What Matters 114
   Your Daily Dare 121

*I dedicate this book to
My mother, Brenda Crockett-Wood
December 5, 1945 – March 23, 2018*

(2 Samuel 12:23)

You are a chosen generation, a royal priesthood, a holy nation, His own special people, that you may proclaim the praises of Him who called you out of darkness into His marvelous light.

−1 Peter 2:9

Introduction

The call of God is, first of all, an invitation to come into the light of the knowledge of Jesus Christ and have a relationship with the Father so you can be the woman He created you to be and live the life He intended for you, one that will glorify Him and bring you joy, fruitfulness, and blessings. And, second, it is an invitation to step into your eternal purpose and do the works He chose, equipped, and appointed you to do.

The first mention of the word *called* is found in the book of Genesis when God divided light from darkness and called the light Day.

> *God created the heavens and the earth. The earth was without form, and void; and darkness was on the face of the deep. And the Spirit*

of God was hovering over the face of the waters. Then God said, 'Let there be light'; and there was light. And God saw the light that it was good, and God divided the light from the darkness. God called the light Day, and the darkness He called Night. So the evening and the morning were the first day. (Genesis 1:1–5 NKJV)

The word translated called in verse five is the Hebrew word "qârâ'." It means to call out, to bid forth, to invite, and to give a name and a purpose.

This is important to remember because the same way God called light (Hebrew: to shine or make manifest, clear, brightness, happiness, day, morning, sun) out of the formless void (Hebrew: purposelessness, confusion, vanity, and undistinguishable emptiness), said it was good, and then divided light from the darkness (Hebrew: misery, destruction, death, sorrow, wickedness, and ignorance) and gave it a name, a purpose, and a beautiful existence is the same way He called you and me.

> 2 Corinthians 4:6 says, For it is the God who commanded light to shine out of darkness, who has shone in our hearts to give the light of the knowledge of the glory of God in the face of Jesus Christ.

When you said yes to God's call and willingly followed Him, He gave you a new identity, a new name, and a purpose so your life can be purposeful and beautiful and prosperous and pleasurable and good.

He commanded the scattering of your soul to come back together again. He set His plan in motion to take away your shame, remove your confusion, and make you who He intended you to be before you were ever born.

However, when God calls us out of darkness into the light of His purpose, most women come out with at least one if not more deep-rooted fears and insecurities founded in issues from the past that no longer defines who we are as God's daughters.

Insecurity is a lack of self-confidence and uncertainty or anxiety about you. Fear is faithlessness rooted in a lack of belief in God's love for you. Fear and insecurity affect your ability to believe you are worthy and capable of being who God called you to be and doing what He called you to do.

Fear and insecurity breed pride and low self-esteem, which in turn, breed comparison and competition. The result is that we compare ourselves to other women constantly. We enter into unspoken competitions with other women, striving to be more, do more, and have more to measure up to the unrealistic goals we set for ourselves. No, we do not call it a competition, not even to ourselves, but it is.

In this age of social media and entertainment overload, the evil seeds of comparison and competition take root through constantly viewing images that paint pictures of perfect lives lived by perfect people we feel we can never have or measure up to. These images don't paint the full picture of the lives we compare our own lives to. Yet, the seeds of competition and comparison grow up to be the thorns that choke God's word and make us unfruitful in our callings (see Mark 4:19 and 2 Peter 1:8).

2 Corinthians 10:12 says, "They, measuring themselves by themselves, and comparing themselves among themselves, are not wise." If you constantly compare yourself to other women, darkness will overshadow you, and you will never be able to see clearly who God called you to be.

If you constantly measure your success and purpose in life by other women's lives, you will never be able to enjoy the life God intended for you. You will never be content with who you are and what you have, and you will compromise who God called you to be to fit into roles God never intended for you.

For a time, longer than I care to admit, I struggled with insecurities and fears. They kept from me seeing myself as God called me to be and from fully stepping into my identity and purpose in Christ. Like most women, my insecurities were rooted in experiences from my past that continued to overshadow my identity after I became a Christian.

Psalm 119:130 says, "The entrance of Your words gives light." Not until I was willing to deal with my fears and insecurities as the light of God's word exposed them in me, was I able to step into the identity and purpose God intended for me.

When we spend time with God in worship, prayer, and meditating on His word, He uncovers our hidden fears, insecurities, and the other issues that hinder us from entering into the plans He has for us. When we believe what He says about us, His words dispel the darkness that surrounds us and shape us into the women He called us to be.

During my times of worship and prayer, the Lord began to speak to me and show me who He called me to be, as well as my purpose and His plans for me. I began to journal what He said to me so that I could speak His words over myself daily. When I realized that He was showing me my God-given calling, I decided to craft a personal calling statement.

A personal calling statement is meant to be a guiding light to help you focus on who God called you to be, and what He called you to do so you won't be distracted and scattered all over the place, unsure of what you should give your time and attention.

Your personal calling consists of your God-given identity, your purpose and mission, vision, your values, and how they will guide you. Crafting a personal calling statement is an act of self-discovery that will help you clarify your God-given calling and give you the confidence and courage to live it.

Courage is not the absence of fear, but the willingness to do what God called you to do in the face of fear. Confidence is faith and certainty in God's ability to do in, and for you what He promised you. Confidence is also being sure of yourself — that you are capable and equipped to do what God has called you to do, simply because He chose you.

Together, courage and confidence will help you overcome fear and insecurity. As you take courage, fear will give way to faith and confidence will open the way for you to walk in your calling.

Getting clear about my personal calling and understanding was the key that unlocked my confidence in what God said about me and allowed me to focus on my purpose and the mission God gave me.

As I developed the habit of affirming my calling statement and believing what God said about me, regardless of what I felt, my past, and what I saw or didn't see in me, His promises began to shape my identity and the way I live my faith. I stopped comparing my life to other women, and I began walking in my calling with confidence and courage.

This blueprint is a step-by-step guide to help you get clear about your God-given your identity, your purpose, and your mission, and to equip you, whatever season you are in to begin walking in your calling.

My prayer is that as you go through the pages of this blueprint and willingly do the work, you would become secure in your identity, assured of your purpose and your mission, and begin walking in your calling with confidence and courage.

CHAPTER 1

Called Out

The apostle Peter explaining to the believers of his day the new identity we are given when God calls us out of darkness wrote these words:

> *But you are a chosen generation, a royal priesthood, a holy nation, His own special people, that you may proclaim the praises of Him who called you out of darkness into His marvelous light. (1 Peter 2:9)*

A closer look at the keywords in this text in the original Greek language reveals the richness of what Peter intended to convey.

You, Beloved, have been favored and selected by God to be a part of His family and live as a royal priest – one who has direct access to God and lives a set-apart life. You are part of a nation whose foundation is God's sovereign power. God has made you morally blameless before Him. He set you apart for Himself.

You are a part of His special race of people whom He bought with the precious blood of Jesus Christ, to make known to others His goodness in calling you by His name out of shadiness, obscurity, shadows, sin, and error into the wonderful clarity and openness of His light.

The Bible refers to darkness as sin over 4800 times. Whatever darkness, shadiness, shadow, error, or sin you were in, however big or small it was in your eyes, whatever you or anyone else labeled your sin, all sin is darkness to God. He called you out to bring you into the light of His purpose and to make you a light in this dark world. You were specially selected and hand-picked by God to be Jesus' witness and make His goodness known in your spheres of influence.

God chose you before the world was established, before you knew right from wrong, before you could commit sin or ask forgiveness for your sins, and before you could choose Him. He chose you — freely according to His own will not because of how good you are but because of His grace and the love He has for you (Ephesians 1:4–5).

Because of His love for you, He desires a relationship with Him. To know God, the Father, and to be known by Him through cultivating an intimate relationship with Him is your first and greatest calling.

As you cultivate your relationship with the Father, He will reveal His purpose and plans for you, and the gifts, talents, and abilities He placed in you so you can fulfill your calling.

On the following page, take some time to list the things God called you out from and how, if at all, they still affect how you see yourself.

This exercise is meant to bring to light any fears or insecurities that are still holding you in bondage to your past so you can overcome them.

You cannot overcome what you are not willing to expose in God's light. What you write is between God and you, so be honest about your struggles.

CALLED OUT

CHAPTER 2

The Heart of the Father

The heart of the Father is that you would have an intimate relationship with Him and be shaped into the image of His Son so that Jesus would not be the only one but the firstborn of many children of God, (Romans 8:29). *John 17:3 says, "This is eternal life, that they may know You, the only true God, and Jesus Christ whom You have sent."* The word *know* in John 17:3, means to be aware of, to feel, to have knowledge of, to perceive, be able to speak of, be sure of, and to understand God.

Eternal life is the reality of knowing God and His Son Jesus, personally. You don't have to wait until you get to heaven to enjoy eternal life. You can enjoy eternal life now through your relationship with God, the Father, the Son, and the Holy Spirit in the present world.

Anything you will ever become or do of eternal value is dependent on your relationship with the Father and how He leads you. As you set your heart to know and worship the Father, He will show you how to follow His plan.

The best way to nurture your connection with the Father and experience an intimate relationship with Him is to worship Him in spirit and truth. Jesus said the Father seeks such worshipers (John 4:24).

To worship in spirit and truth is to seek God with the awareness that your every thought and the intentions of your heart is exposed in the light of His presence, and yet to unreservedly yield your will to Him and allow Him to shape every area of your life after His will as you surrender to Him.

God's L.A.B.

All women have three God-given desires that must be met to thrive emotionally and relationally: a desire to experience unconditional love, a desire to be accepted for who we really are, and a desire to feel beautiful. At the core of these desires is the inborn image of God within us. He is Love, He is the Grantor of eternal acceptance, and He is the Beautiful One.

When we worship in His presence and stay in communion with the Father, He shapes our identities through the transforming power of His love, acceptance, and beauty, what I like to call God's L.A.B.

Love

You are loved by God, perfectly and completely. In this life, our ability to understand God's perfect, unfailing love for us is limited by our human perception. However, unlike our idea of completeness or perfection that can be undone, broken, or changed, His love cannot and will not change. It is complete now and forever. The Father can never love you more than He does right now. There is nothing you can do or that you have to do to earn His love or to receive more of it.

In the same way, there is nothing you can do to make the Father love you any less. On your best day, God doesn't love you anymore, and on your worst day, He doesn't love you any less. His love remains the same. It never weakens or stops working.

The Father has obligated His love to remain the same through all of life's seasons like an ember that refuses to burn out. In the good times, the Father's love is like the flicker burning atop a sweet-scented candle. It fills the atmosphere with joy and happiness, and it brings comfort and rest. In the hard times, His love is like the fire that led the children of Israel through the wilderness, fierce and sure, a shield of protection in danger.

As you learn to trust in the Father's love, it will drive out all fear, shame, and brokenness. In exchange, His love will give you faith, courage, love for others, and make you free to be who He called you to be.

Acceptance

You are accepted by God. The Father's acceptance is more than being admitted into a clique or a club. His acceptance is being specially chosen in love without pretense and having grace, honor, and abundant favor bestowed upon you by the One who chose you.

It is no coincidence that Paul chose to use the same Greek word *charitoo* to express to believers that we are "accepted in the Beloved" (Ephesians 1:6), as Luke used when he described the angel Gabriel telling Mary she had been highly favored. *"And having come in, the angel said to her, 'Rejoice, highly favored one, the Lord is with you; blessed are you among women!'"* (Luke 1:26–28).

The word *charitoo* means to have grace, to be clothed with special honor, to make accepted, and to be highly favored. When Paul said we are "accepted in the Beloved," he was saying that in Christ, we have been granted the same grace, acceptance, honor, and favor God gave Mary when He chose her to bring forth the Messiah.

Mary was no different from any other young Jewish woman. She said of herself, *"The Lord has looked upon the lowly" (Luke 1:48).* The Lord chose Mary not because she was better than anyone else, but out of the counsel and delight of His own will. That is the same reason He chose you and me.

The Father's acceptance does away with insecurities, comparison, low self-esteem, and trying to fit in. In exchange, it makes you confident and accepting of yourself. His acceptance causes His favor to rest upon you, and it leads you to the people and the places He has prepared for you. When you believe that the Father has accepted, you will see yourself as worthy of all He wants to do in, for, and through you.

Beauty

You are beautiful. God created women altogether beautiful — on the inside and the outside. He perfectly knit each one of us together — body, features, and hue, to fit our individual and unique identities. He put a distinct purpose in each of us when He called us so that we can each display His beauty in our unique ways.

He planted the seed of His incorruptible, everlasting beauty in our hearts so our attitudes can be a reflection of His beauty as we allow the seed to grow.

> *1Peter 3:3-4 said, Do not let your adornment be merely outward—arranging the hair, wearing gold, or putting on fine apparel— rather let it be the hidden person of the heart, with the*

incorruptible beauty of a gentle and quiet spirit, which is very precious in the sight of God.

This God-kind of beauty referred to as *na'om* in the Old Testament has the same root word used in Naomi's name, who was the mother-in-law of Ruth. It is the same word King David used to describe the Lord's beauty:

One thing have I desired of the Lord and that one thing will I seek, that I may dwell in the house of the Lord all the days of my life to behold the beauty of the Lord, and to inquire in His temple. (Psalm 27:4)

The full meaning of the word is agreeableness, splendor, kindness, delightfulness, perfection, majesty, grace, and pleasantness. This beauty is spiritual, just as God is a Spirit.

Naomi, at one point in her life, asked people to call her Mara, because she believed the Lord had dealt her a bitter hand in life. The name *Mara* comes from the Hebrew word bitter, and means to be angry, irritated, unhappy, unpleasant, and weighed down (see Ruth 1:20). It is the opposite of the God-kind of beauty.

Naomi allowed the things that happened to her to overshadow her God-given identity. However, God never called her Mara because Naomi remained beautiful in the eyes of the Lord. However, she had to decide to choose beauty over bitterness in spite of what had happened to her. As soon as she started to focus on the beauty in front of her instead of the pain of her past, she felt like herself again: beautiful and pleasant.

This is the kind of beauty the Lord wants you to choose so you can be shaped in your identity to be a reflection of His beauty as the woman He called you to be.

The more time you spend with the Lord beholding His beauty, the more His beauty will influence you and begin to change your attitude to make you a reflection of His kindness, delightfulness, perfection, majesty, grace and pleasantness, and beauty.

Your Spiritual Blessings and Inheritance

As God's daughter, not only was His love, acceptance, and beauty bestowed on you, but He has blessed you with spiritual blessings and an inheritance.

Ephesians 1:3 tells us that we have been *"blessed us with every spiritual blessing in the heavenly places in Christ."*

The word blessing in this verse is a translation of the Greek word eulogy, and it means to speak well of, to pronounce, and invoke good things that cause one to prosper.

The good things that God has decreed for you are probably beyond your ability to number, but Ephesians 1: 4-14 outlines a few of them.

As I've already noted, He chose you before He established the world. He made you holy and blameless.

He preordained you to be His daughter through adoption by Jesus Christ. He made you accepted.

He paid the cost for your ransom from sin, death, and hell with the blood of His Son. Instead of judgment, by the riches of His grace, He has completely forgiven your sins, now and forever.

He has graciously given you every kind of wisdom and insight. All you have to do is ask (James 1:6). The mystery of His will has been opened to you through Christ. These are the good things God has granted you and spoken about you for your good, to see you prosper. Though they are spiritual, they will work themselves out in your natural life when you accept them as true, believe they are yours, and walk in the reality of the power of what was bestowed on you.

God also gave you an inheritance in Christ, and He sealed you with the Holy Spirit as a guarantee of your eternal inheritance until you enter the fullness thereof in the life to come.

Ephesians 1:11 says, *"In Him also we have obtained an inheritance, being predestined according to the purpose of Him who works all things according to the counsel of His will."*

The word inheritance in this text means to give a portion, to allot, to assign a privilege, also a birthright. You have obtained an inheritance as your birthright, and you now possess all the benefits of salvation offered in Christ. These benefits of salvation are also too many to count. However, all that God promised in His word to those who believe in Jesus Christ is yours, in this life and the life to come.

The apostle Peter further describes the nature of this inheritance, saying that we have been born again *"to an inheritance incorruptible and undefiled, and that does not fade away, reserved in heaven for you."* (1 Peter 1:4)

Your God-given inheritance can never perish. It is not subject to corruption or decay. It cannot be spoiled, tainted, or made impure. It is everlasting.

You received it the minute you were born again; however, the full redemption of your inheritance is held safely in heaven, awaiting your arrival.

CHAPTER 3

Handpicked

The apostle Paul writing to the church of Rome, described himself in the following manner: *"Paul, a bondservant of Jesus Christ, called to be an apostle, separated to the gospel of God,"* (Romans 1:1).

The word *called* in this verse means to be appointed to something specific. God chose Paul to *be* an apostle long before he was ever born or heard Jesus call his name. When Paul said yes to God's call, God set him apart on a course to fulfill the purpose He appointed to him.

Luke, the writer of the book of Acts, went further in his clarification of Paul's calling. Using a special word, *procheirizomai* in Greek, only found twice in the New Testament, he described how God chose

Paul for His work. Not because Paul was more special than any of the other apostles but because he wanted to express God's predetermined purpose in choosing each one of us.

The first occurrence of the word is found in Acts 22:14,

> *Then he said, 'The God of our fathers has chosen you that you should know His will, and see the Just One, and hear the voice of His mouth.'*

Here the word is translated as "chosen."

The second occurrence is found in Acts 26:16,

> *But rise and stand on your feet; for I have appeared to you for this purpose, to make you a minister and a witness both of the things which you have seen and of the things which I will yet reveal to you.*

In this verse, the word is translated as "to make."

The word means to be handpicked by God, to pre-purpose in advance, to handle for one's self, to make or to choose.

God handpicks us, and then He shapes us according to the pre-purposed work, whatever that may be, that He created and chose us to do. Not according to what our circumstances say or what the world concludes, not according to our qualifications but according to His grace and His plan.

God took Paul, someone who at one time never thought he would have become a Christian, let alone an apostle, and made him a messenger to the Gentiles.

Paul was a pureblooded Hebrew. He was a Pharisee — a very religious Jewish man who separated himself from non-Jews. He thought the very idea of Jesus was blasphemous because of the inclusion He came to preach, that by grace through faith in His name, all men could be saved and have a part in the covenant made to Abraham.

Paul thought he was doing God a favor by persecuting the church. He went around rounding up Christians to have them killed. Jesus called Paul while he was on his way to persecute Christians, the very people he hated, and spoke to him about the work He had chosen him to do.

Saul from Tarsus, became Paul, an apostle, not to Jewish or religious people but Gentiles. Paul became a person that could be all things to all people that he might win some to Christ (1 Corinthians 9:22). This goes to show that God chooses whomever He wants to do His will. Your calling is not based on things that can be boxed into a figureoutable formula.

The mystery of God's calling is that He often calls us to do things we do not feel qualified or equipped to do. However, there is a special sense of purpose that comes from experiencing God's providence in your life, having to depend on Him, knowing you cannot brag about what you have done but only boast in God.

1 Corinthians 1:24–31 says,

But to those who are called, both Jews and Greeks, Christ the power of God and the wisdom of God. Because the foolishness of God is wiser than men, and the weakness of God is stronger than men. For you see your calling, brethren, that not many wise according to the flesh, not many mighty, not many noble, are called. But God has chosen the foolish things of the world to put to shame the wise, and God has chosen the weak things of the world to put to shame the things which are mighty; and the base things of the world and the things which are despised God has chosen, and the things which are not, to bring to nothing the things that are, that no flesh should glory in His presence. But of Him you are in Christ Jesus, who became for us wisdom from God—and righteousness and sanctification and redemption— that, as it is written, 'He who glories, let him glory in the Lord.'

Paul wrote those words after he experienced God's power at work in His own life. This man who once persecuted Christians is responsible for writing over half the New Testament. He brought the gospel for the first time to several Gentile groups. He had dreams and visions, some of which he could not even speak, (2 Corinthians 12:1-6).

He wasn't able to do these things because of his power, might, wisdom, and insight. God gifted, anointed, and equipped this man who had before been extremely religious but ordinary to do these works because God handpicked him for the works.

Like Paul, God may have chosen you to do something you never thought you would do. He may have chosen you to minister to people that are very unlike you and what you are accustomed to.

On the other hand, God may have chosen you to reach people who are similar to you and have had similar experiences that you can relate to. Whatever the case, you can be certain your calling is not a mistake. He handpicked you to fulfill your part in His plan.

Your Spiritual Gifts

When God handpicked you, He gave you spiritual gifts to help equip you to do the things He chose you to do. However, He also made it so that you must rely on the Holy Spirit's empowerment for your gifts to work effectively.

Some spiritual gifts are miraculous. Some are natural abilities that God enhances with the supernatural capability to do things with such skillfulness that you know it is Him working through you to will and to do His good pleasure (Philippians 2:13).

All spiritual gifts, whether miraculous or natural, work by the Holy Spirit. Paul listed the various gifts throughout the New Testament texts.

> *1 Corinthians 12:4-11 says, There are diversities of gifts, but the same Spirit. There are differences of ministries, but the same Lord. And*

there are diversities of activities, but it is the same God who works all in all. But the manifestation of the Spirit is given to each one for the profit of all: for to one is given the word of wisdom through the Spirit, to another the word of knowledge through the same Spirit, to another faith by the same Spirit, to another gifts of healings by the same Spirit, to another the working of miracles, to another prophecy, to another discerning of spirits, to another different kinds of tongues, to another the interpretation of tongues. But one and the same Spirit works all these things, distributing to each one individually as He wills.

Romans 12:4-8 says, For as we have many members in one body, but all the members do not have the same function, so we, being many, are one body in Christ, and individually members of one another. Having then gifts differing according to the grace that is given to us, let us use them: if prophecy, let us prophesy in proportion to our faith; or ministry, let us use it in our ministering; he who teaches, in teaching; he who exhorts, in exhortation; he who gives, with liberality; he who leads, with diligence; he who shows mercy, with cheerfulness.

Ephesians 4:11-13 says, He Himself gave some to be apostles, some prophets, some evangelists, and some pastors and teachers, for the equipping of the saints for the work of ministry, for the edifying of the body of Christ, till we all come to the unity of the faith and of the knowledge of the Son of God, to a perfect man, to the measure of the stature of the fullness of Christ.

Discovering your gifts is a process that happens over time. As you yield to the Holy Spirit, make yourself available to Him, and for service to others, your spiritual gifts will be revealed to you. All you have to do is yield to Him, and He will help you unwrap the gifts He has placed on the inside of you.

Some spiritual gifts, like those listed in Ephesians, are meant to equip the saints for the work of the ministry. Other spiritual gifts are meant to be a witness of Christ's power and love to those that are still in darkness. But no one gift is better than the others. All gifts, as all the members of the body, are needed for the body of Christ to function properly. (1 Corinthians 12:12-30)

Honor your gifts because God gave them to you, and the body of Christ you are connected to needs them to flow through you. Whatever role God has called you to in His kingdom, your spiritual gifts are meant to help equip you to do the work God has called you to do.

However, God doesn't want you to get caught up in the hype of having gifts. Remain focused on the gift Giver, serving others as unto the Lord, and your gifts will make room for you.

If you already know what they are or even if you are not sure but only have an idea, on the next page, list your spiritual gifts.

For example, God called me to be an evangelist. He has granted me the gifts preaching and teaching His word, praying, prophesying, giving words of knowledge, and praying for the sick. I am also a leader, a writer, and an administrator /organizer using the natural abilities that the Holy Spirit enhances in me.

Krista Pettiford

CHAPTER 4

Called to Be Authentic

When I first became a Christian, I did not feel like I measured up to the other Christian women around me. I had been a teenage mother, and I found myself going through a divorce with four small children after I gave my life to Christ. However, despite all of my self-doubt and insecurities, soon after I joined my church, the Lord began to call me into ministry. I had no idea what was expected of me, so I began to try to be like the other women around me.

Then one day, while I was worshiping the Lord, He spoke to me with a still small voice and said, *"I desire an authentic relationship with you. Do not come into my presence with pretense. You cannot build an authentic relationship with me unless you come to me genuinely. Do not try to change who you are. I knew who you were when I called you."* Those words changed my life, my perspective of God, and how I saw myself.

The word authentic means true, genuine, honest, reliable, and trustworthy. It wasn't that God did not expect me to take off my old nature and put on Christ. He wanted me to walk in my new identity in Christ, but genuinely as the woman He called me to be. He revealed the things I needed to do away with that would hinder me from spiritual maturity.

You do not have to pretend to be someone you are not with God. He wants you to have an authentic relationship with Him, knowing that He sees the real you and loves and accepts you.

If God wanted everyone to be alike, look alike, and sound alike, He could have easily created us that way. But He chose instead to make each one of us as unique as our fingerprints so He could tell us apart and enjoy us as individuals.

Psalm 139:14 says, "I will praise You, for I am fearfully and wonderfully made." The Hebrew word fearfully used in this verse means reverential. The word wonderfully means to distinguish, to set apart, to show or make a difference between individuals. God put thought into making each one of us wonderfully unique and different from each other. However, He made sure we would have to come together on the common ground of His sacred unifying grace.

The realization that I did not have to pretend to be someone or something I'm not to have a relationship with God or to serve Him allowed me to have an authentic relationship with the God who sees me knows me and wants to have a relationship with me.

When I realized that I did not have to be the perfect image of who I thought God wanted me to be, I gained the freedom to grow into the authentic image of Christ as the woman God called me to be.

God knows your story. He knows the things you are going through right now. He chose you before you were born. He loved you and accepted you before you ever knew Him. Not in spite of who you are, but because of who you are through faith in His Son.

The Lord will use all of your experiences to shape you into the woman He called you to be so that you can be a witness to other women in your generation. So other women can relate to you and feel at ease being transparent with you, and you can have compassion on them because you can relate to them. So you can lead others who are standing where you've been — out of darkness and into God's light.

Don't be ashamed of your past or even what you're going through right now. Other women need you to be authentic and secure in your identity. Your lights shine brighter and more brilliantly when you are comfortable in your own identity, and you allow yourself to be who God called you to be.

For me, being authentic means showing up for life without fear or pretense or measuring my identity by the ruler of women's lives.

On the next page, list the things about you and your story that are unique. Then define what being authentic means to you. How can these things help you be a better witness for Jesus?

Krista Pettiford

CHAPTER 5

Your Purpose and Your Mission

Though your purpose and mission are knit together, they are not the same. It is important to understand the difference because many people know their purpose but do not understand how to carry out their mission effectively, so they never fulfill their purpose. Your mission is what you do. Your purpose is why you do it.

Your purpose goes beyond your mission. It is God's intention for you, and the end He had in mind when He called and chose you. It is the completion of your faith, His plan for you, and the reason you were born again. Everyone is born with a purpose, but not everyone will fulfill his or her purpose and make it to God's intended end.

Jesus is an example of someone who understood His purpose and His mission.

Purpose

1 John 3:8 says, "For this purpose the Son of God was manifested, that He might destroy the works of the devil." The word used for *purpose* in 1 John 3:8 means intent or the reason for which someone or something exists. Jesus' purpose was to destroy the works of the devil. That was the reason He came into the world.

Romans 8:28 says, "We know that for those who love God all things work together for good, for those who are called according to his purpose." Here Paul uses another word that is the Greek equivalent for the Hebrew word *showbread* or *Bread of the Presence*.

It means a setting forth as the showbread in the Temple is exposed before God. It also means a plan or an intention. This bread was present in the Presence of God at all times. It was left on the table for a week and then replaced with new loaves every Sabbath so that there were always fresh loaves on the table. The loaves that started going stale were removed.

The showbread is a reminder that God calls us for His purpose, not our own. Therefore, we must stay connected to Him in prayer and depend on Him to receive His new instructions if we are to fulfill our part in His plan. And, as we do, He promises to make everything we go through work for our good.

Mission

Speaking about Jesus, Hebrews 10:7 says, *"Then I said, 'Behold, I have come — in the volume of the book it is written of Me — to do Your will, O God."* The word used for do in Hebrews 10:7 means to execute, to fulfill, to perform, or to carry out (as in a mission). It is the same word used in Ephesians 2:10 to describe the works God created us to do.

Jesus knew that focusing on His mission — the daily work the Father called Him to do, would lead to the fulfillment of His purpose.

Jesus' mission was to do the will of the Father as the Father revealed it to Him.

> In John 5:19, Jesus said, "Most assuredly, I say to you, the Son can do nothing of Himself, but what He sees the Father do; for whatever He does, the Son also does in like manner."

By staying connected to the Father's presence, Jesus received the spiritual strength necessary to submit to the Father's will and only do what He saw His Father do, according to the Father's purpose and plan.

> Mark 1:25 says, "Rising very early in the morning, while it was still dark, he departed and went out to a desolate place, and there he prayed."

Jesus' consistent times of prayer helped prepare Him for His greatest mission and the ultimate act of submission — giving His life on the cross for the sins of the world and in doing so fulfilling His purpose on earth by destroying the works of the devil.

Jesus did many mighty works, but they all led to the same purpose — to undo the works of the devil. Like

Jesus, your mission is to do the good works you were created to do. Your purpose is to accomplish your part — whatever it is that God reveals to you in His plan.

Like Jesus, the way you carry out your mission can and will change as you go through different seasons in life, but your purpose will remain the same.

You may be single or married. You may be a stay-at-home mom or a work-from-home mom or an empty nester. You may be in between jobs. You may be an entrepreneur by design or forced hand. You may be working a job and your dream at the same time. You may be called to full-time ministry, or you may be called to of all these things at the same time or in different seasons.

Whether it's going back to work after having a child, staying home with children after working outside the home, taking a lesser paying job, taking on more responsibility in your job, starting a business, or caring for a loved one, it can be difficult to understand how to carry out your mission when your season changes.

There will be seasons that make you feel like your dreams are on hold and seasons when you feel you don't have enough energy and time to do everything in front of you.

The good news is that godly success is measured by your obedience to the will of God. The only thing that matters is that you do the work He calls you to do, one day at a time and one act of obedience at a time.

You can do God's will in any season of life if you understand that you are called according to His purpose and plans, and you learn to submit to His will readily. The Holy Spirit will guide you to each new assignment and show you how to carry out your mission.

When I was starting in ministry, God spoke directly to my heart and said, "I have called you to be an evangelist." However, I did not immediately step into my calling as an evangelist. I had four small children who needed my time and attention. Also, God was still preparing me to walk in my calling. However, I hid His word in my heart and began studying Timothy, whom Paul instructed to do the work of an evangelist.

When I finally began to walk in my calling as an evangelist, I realized that whatever other roles in life I've had or have now, as a wife, mother, sister, friend, or servant-leader, career woman, business owner, writer and creative, I am also called to preach the gospel.

No matter what season of life or role I'm in, I'm always aware of my mission is to do the work of the ministry, by sharing the messages God has given me, to make Jesus known, and to win souls. By submitting to God's will and looking to Him for instructions, I have learned to be satisfied with only doing what He calls me to do.

You fulfill your calling in God's kingdom by submitting to Him and allowing Him to show you how to use your gifts, talents, and abilities for His glory each day and in each new season, whether you affect one person at a time, few, or many.

I believe this is what Paul meant when he urged believers to redeem the time (Ephesians 5:16). Redeeming the time means to buy up or take advantage of every opportunity to do good works that God (not man) presents to you.

On the next two pages, clarify your why — the purpose for which you believe God called you, and your what – the mission (good works) you believe God is calling you to do in this season. Include how you believe God wants you to carry out the goods work in this season.

CALLED OUT

CHAPTER 6

Your God-given Dreams and Visions

God created you with a specific plan in mind. He can reveal His plans for you in any way He chooses. However, of the many ways He could, God often chooses to use dreams and visions to reveal what He has planned for you.

The Bible defines a vision as a mental image, a sight, a dream, or a revelation from God that foretells the plans He has for you. These types of visions are prophetic. However, God also plants His eternal plans in our hearts as seeds of hope for our future to anchor our faith in His promises. (Ecclesiastes 3:11)

To some people, He reveals His plans little by little. Yet, He shows other people the big picture, what the Bible calls, "the end from the beginning" (Isaiah 46:10) at once.

Most God-given dreams and visions, whether great or small, are bigger than what you can think or imagine on your own. They are bigger than what you can do on your own or even with the help of other people. They require God's divine assistance.

According to Habakkuk 2:2, when the Lord gives you a vision or plants a dream in your heart, the next step is to *"Write the vision."*

The prophets of Israel wrote with vivid detail many things the Lord spoke to them and showed them. The apostles of the early church wrote letters to remember what was spoken and shown to them as well. The prophets and the apostles did this not just for themselves but for those who would come after them. We have the words of the Old and New Covenants because the prophets and the apostles wrote what God by His Spirit showed and told them.

The Lord instructed the prophet Habakkuk to *"make it plain on tablets,"* so those who were running the race of faith could easily see it, read it, and understand it quickly and clearly, and be encouraged in their faith to keep going.

> *Habakkuk 2:3 says, "For the vision is yet for an appointed time; but at the end it will speak, and it will not lie. Though it tarries, wait for it; because it will surely come, it will not tarry."*

Having a written vision that you can easily see and read will encourage your faith and help you wait patiently for God's plans to happen in your life.

You should write your vision and make it visually easy to read and understand, using pictures as well as words because mental images fade with time, even when they are from God. But pictures and written words will help you remember what was spoken and shown to you by the Lord.

Prayer is a vital part of the process of receiving God-given visions. Habakkuk was in prayer when the Lord showed him the vision, *"I will stand my watch and set myself on the wall, and watch to see what He will say to me," (Habakkuk 2:1).* Your dreams and visions will become clearer over time as God reveals more of His plans to you.

The biggest obstacle your dreams and visions will face is you believing what God shows you. Even if what He shows you seem impossible to you, write your visions and your dreams anyway. Place your written dreams and vision somewhere you can see them, easily read them, be encouraged by them, and live intentionally in the direction they point you.

Write Your Vision

The following is a list of the steps God gave me when I created my first vision board. I still use them today. These steps have helped many other women write their visions and create vision boards.

1. Get into a prayerful state and settle your soul to its quiet place so you can focus inwardly and see what God wants to show you. Take every thought captive that says you can't do, be, have, experience what God shows you.

2. Don't Hold Back! Write whatever God says to you and shows you. Also, write the desires of your heart: the things you want to be, do, see, have, and experience. As you learn to trust God and understand His plan for you to have a blessed life, your vision will become bigger!

3. Prayerfully consider if the desires of your heart align with God's will for you. Some things will not align, other things will be for another time, and yet, other things God will encourage you to pursue now.

4. If necessary, rewrite your vision.

5. Look for corresponding scripture verses to include to support your vision.

6. Based on what you have written, write clear and concise, present tense declarations that will help you envision yourself living in your dreams and visions.

7. If you choose to make a vision board from your written vision, find images that will help you see yourself as already being, doing, and having what God showed you. Paste them to your board with your declarations and scriptures.

CALLED OUT

Krista Pettiford

CHAPTER 7

Craft Your Motto

A personal motto is meant to be the light that guides your feet, just as Psalm 119:105 tells us that God's word is *"a lamp to our feet and a light to our path."*

A motto is a core value or principle concisely and consistently expressed that reinforces the concepts you already believe. It represents a fundamental belief that helps shape your behavior as you try to live up to the mission it represents.

A personal motto is meant to be a phrase you begin to live your life around. However, without a sense of personal conviction, your motto won't mean much. But if a motto is used as a reminder of the bigger picture of your beliefs, purpose, mission, and vision, it can be a powerful tool to help you live out your calling.

You can have more than one motto. Some people have a motto for each area of life. Your motto may change as you go through different seasons in life.

My motto was "Joy is strength" (Nehemiah 8:10) during the time I went through my divorce, and for several years after the divorce was final.

Rehearsing those words helped me live my life around the truth they represented. God's joy became my strength in that very hard season, and I was able to keep an attitude of grace and gratitude for myself and my children.

Personal My mottos over the years:
Joy is strength
Perfect love cast our fear
Preach, prophesy, pray.

Personal mottos by other people:
"Darkness cannot drive out darkness: only light can do that. Hate cannot drive out hate: only love can do that."–Martin Luther King, Jr.

"If God is your partner, make your plans BIG!" –D.L. Moody

"Be faithful in small things because it is in them that your strength lies." –Mother Teresa

Organizational mottos:

"Never Again" - Jewish Defense League

"Pray and work" - Benedictine Order

"Always faithful" - US Marines

"Truth" - Harvard University

"Be prepared" - Boy Scouts

Nations:

"In God We Trust" - USA

Unity and Faith, Peace and Progress" – Nigeria

"Liberty, equality, fraternity" - France

United in diversity" - European Union

Write Your Motto

On the next page, to craft your motto, first look for a scripture that expresses the value, principle, or belief you want to live your life around. If you cannot find a scripture, write down a few words or a statement that embodies the belief or principle you want your motto to represent.

Keep it short: a simple word, phrase, or sentence will do.

CALLED OUT

CHAPTER 8

Craft Your Calling Statement

A personal calling statement is comprised of your best understanding to date of what God has called you to be and do: your God-given identity, your purpose and mission, your vision, your values and how they will guide you — all the things we've covered so far in this blueprint. Now it's time to put all the pieces together to craft your personal calling statement.

Your calling statement should provide clarity and define who you are and how you will live. It should be easy to understand and to the point.

Here are a few benefits of creating a personal calling statement.

1. It integrates who you are and what you are called to do.
2. It provides focus so you can live a more intentional life.
3. It acts as a compass to guide you on your path.
4. It simplifies any decision-making processes and holds you accountable for your decisions.

To create your calling statement, answer the following questions:

Identity: Who are you? What roles and responsibilities have God given you? What makes you unique?

Gifts: What spiritual gifts, skills, and abilities had God given you?

Purpose: For what purpose do you believe God called you? What are you called to fulfill?

Mission: What are the good works God created you to do? What are your aspirations, and what are you passionate about?

Vision: What dreams and visions have God placed in your heart?

Values: Who and what matters to you? What are your convictions and the beliefs you want to guide you?

Write Your Calling Statement:

Look for the common thread in everything you wrote. Then complete the following statements.

I am called to be:

My life purpose is to:

My mission is to:

As I live out my purpose and mission, these values will guide me:

My vision is to:

So that...

Lord, as you have called and chosen me, let me live according to your will. Amen.

You may have to write your calling statement more than once as your understanding of your calling becomes clearer.

If you recognized a common thread or word in what you wrote, write it down. It may be a clue to something bigger that God is calling you to do. It may be a word or phrase that can become a motto to guide you.

CHAPTER 9

Reject False Mindsets

Before you can walk confidently in your calling, you have to believe that you are worthy and capable of being, doing, and having all God has promised you in His word. To do that, you have to reject the false mindsets that shaped your thinking before God called you.

Think of your mind like a file cabinet with several folders filled with sets of instructions for how to process all of life's issues. These instructions are mindsets.

A mindset is an established set of attitudes and beliefs held by someone. Mindsets are formed when certain attitudes and beliefs are embraced and allowed to take root in your heart and mind. Most mindsets are rooted in things we were taught and experiences that happened early in life. Mindsets affect the way you process things, your decision-making, and the standards you use to judge yourself and others.

Romans 12:2 says, "Do not be conformed to this world, be transformed by the renewing of your mind, that you may prove what is the good, acceptable, and perfect will of God."

Erroneous mindsets originate in false thoughts, the lies of the devil, and flawed information that, at times, is passed off as truth, traditions, and principles. However, any mindset that does not align with the word and will of God is erroneous.

Erroneous mindsets enforce themselves through reasoning, arguments, and the opinions of your carnal mind, which is set against the knowledge of God(God's will for you). The devil uses erroneous mindsets to limit and control people and to keep them stuck in the same cycles of defeat.

Erroneous mindsets will keep you conformed to the world's way of dealing with the issues of life so that God's transformation is not able to be completed in you and you cannot experience the perfect will of God for your life.

Erroneous mindsets are how strongholds form. A stronghold is a false mindset that has taken control of your reasoning and your thinking so that the truth concerning God's will cannot breakthrough into your thoughts and the way you process information about the issues of life and the things you go through.

Strongholds must be pulled down and destroyed (2 Corinthians 10:4–6) by challenging erroneous mindsets with the truth found in God's word. To do this, you have to pay attention to your thoughts. Then capture and replace any false thoughts with God's word, accepting as true what He says about you.

However, don't be fooled; you can have the right mindsets in one area of life and be bound by erroneous mindsets in another. For example, you can believe that God loves you and, therefore, that you are worthy of love from others. This mindset will produce healthy, loving relationships in your life because you believe and accept as true that love is God's will for you.

On the other hand, if you do not believe that you are capable or worthy of doing what God called you to do, you may enjoy fruitful loving relationships with people whom you connect. But, you will not reach the full potential of your purpose or experience the fullness of the good and perfect will of God in your life.

God wants you to experience all that He planned for you, and renewing your mind is the first step. It takes practice, but with time and consistency, the truth will breakthrough. When it does, truth will become a stronghold of its own against erroneous mindsets and the lies of the enemy.

These strongholds become the cabinets and the file folders that hold truth and spiritual, godly reasoning to filter all the issues of life, good or bad through.

When you believe what God says about you, you begin to see yourself as He sees you, and this is what transforms you and produces God's perfect will in your life.

Replace Lies With Truth

On the next page, skipping a line after each one, list any negative, self-defeating thoughts contrary to what God says about your relationship with Him, your identity, your calling, and His plans for you. Read each negative, self-defeating thought/lie aloud.

Next, write the truth: what God says about you under each false thought/ lie you wrote. Then put a line through each negative statement and read aloud only what God's word says about you.

Finally, on a clean piece of paper, only write what God says about you. Use this truth as your weapon to tear down strongholds, to begin renewing your mind, and against the enemy when he whispers his lies to you.

CALLED OUT

Krista Pettiford

CHAPTER 10

Say What God Says About You

Words believed and spoken, have the creative power to change our lives and our circumstances. Jesus said, *"out of the abundance of the heart the mouth speaks" (Matthew 12:34).* If your heart is filled with fear, your words will be too, and the things you speak in fear may happen, especially if you believe what you say (Job 3:25 and Mark 11:23). Likewise, the things you speak in faith will happen if you believe what you say and it is God's will for you (1 John 5:14-15)

For the longest time after God called me, I was afraid to say what I knew He had spoken to me. I was afraid other people would judge me by my past, my divorce, or one of the many other things that made me feel unworthy of God's calling. I certainly was not prepared to call myself an evangelist or act as if I had a call on my life. I did not have enough confidence or courage to say what God said about me.

Throughout my fear-filled years, God, in His faithfulness, continued to work on me. Despite my fears and playing small, the Holy Spirit began working through me, and my God-given gifts began to make room for me. Eventually, I overcame my fears and began walking my calling.

But first, I had to learn not to allow fear and insecurities to control what I say about me. Looking back, I realize my faith in God's word needed time to grow and create in me the confidence I needed to believe God, be willing to say what He said about me, and not care what other people think.

Like Abraham, the patriarch of our faith, I had to put my hope in God's promises and call myself what He called me so the power of His word could be released in my life.

Romans 4:17-18 says, As it is written, 'I have made you a father of many nations' in the presence of Him whom he believed — God, who gives life to the dead and calls those things which do not exist as though they did; who, contrary to hope, in hope believed, so that he became the father of many nations, according to what was spoken, 'So shall your descendants be.'

Abraham was seventy-five years old when God called him out of his country. At that time, his name was Abram, which means high father.

Genesis 12:1-2 says, Now the Lord had said to Abram: 'Get out of your country, from your family and from your father's house to a land that I will show you. I will make you a great nation; I will bless you and make your name great, and you shall be a blessing.'

Many years after Abram had left his family and his country, and his confidence in God was established, the Lord showed Abraham how he would bring the promise to pass.

> *But Abram said, 'Lord God, what will You give me, seeing I go childless, and the heir of my house is Eliezer of Damascus?' Then Abram said, 'Look, You have given me no offspring; indeed one born in my house is my heir!' And behold, the word of the Lord came to him, saying, 'This one shall not be your heir, but one who will come from your own body shall be your heir.' Then He brought him outside and said, 'Look now toward heaven, and count the stars if you are able to number them.' And He said to him, 'So shall your descendants be.'*
> *(Genesis 15:2-14)*

But Sarai was barren, and she believed her barrenness was too impossible, even for God, to change. She was willing to settle for what she could do on her own to get for herself what God had already granted her. She did not yet know that acting in faith in God's promises could change her life and her circumstance.

So instead of trusting in God's promise and waiting for Him to fulfill His plan in His timing, she devised a plan of her own. She instructed Abram to lay with Hagar, who was her maid, so that Hagar could have a child for them. But the child would belong to Sarai. He did, and they named him Ishmael.

Ishmael was not the child of promise. He was the result of what Sarai and Abram could do on their own to try to fulfill God's plan without His power and outside of His timing. (Genesis 17:20-21)

However, God was determined to fulfill His promise because He is faithful to His word even when we are not. So He went to Abram again at a later time with further instructions.

He instructed Abram, who was ninety-nine by that time to begin calling himself Abraham: father of a multitude (what God called him to be) openly. More specifically, Abraham meant the father of a great nation, for that was the promise. The Lord also changed Sarai's name from Princess to Sarah, which means Queen, for that was who He predestined her to be.

> *No longer shall your name be called Abram, but your name shall be Abraham; for I have made you a father of many nations... Then God said to Abraham, "'As for Sarai your wife, you shall not call her name Sarai, but Sarah shall be her name. (Genesis 17:5 and 15.)*

God knew that if Abraham began to call Sarah and himself what He called them even though what God said seemed impossible, they would become what God called them to be.

After they had called themselves what God called them for a time, the Lord appeared to them again and foretold Isaac's birth, *"At the appointed time I will return to you, according to the time of life, and Sarah shall have a son," (Genesis 18:14).*

Sarah laughed because she still thought what God said was impossible. But the next year, just like God spoke, Sarah had a son and named him Isaac, which means laughter.

Abraham became not just a father, what he could do, but the father of a great nation — the promise of God — more than he could ask or imagine. Sarah became the mother of a great nation — more than she dared to believe.

When we allow fear to control what we do and say, it leads us to detours and delays. God did not want me to pass my years being too afraid to call myself what He called me. God doesn't want you to be afraid, either. Nor does He want you to delay the progress of your purpose by trying to work out His plan on your own. He doesn't want you to settle for only what you can do.

Abraham believed what God said, and even when he made mistakes, he received correction and continued to obey God's instructions.

Romans 4:18-22 says of Abraham:

Contrary to hope, in hope believed, so that he became the father of many nations, according to what was spoken, 'So shall your descendants be.' And not being weak in faith, he did not consider his own body, already dead (since he was about a hundred years old), and the deadness of Sarah's womb. He did not waver at the promise of God through unbelief, but was strengthened in faith, giving glory to God, and being fully convinced that what He had promised He was also able to perform. And therefore 'it was accounted to him for righteousness.'

Beloved, the promise of your calling will not happen overnight. But if you are willing to give God the glory by saying what God says about you even when things look impossible, God will perform His word, and you will become what He called you.

CHAPTER 11

Take Courage

Timothy, a son in the faith to the Apostle Paul, was called to be an evangelist. However, he had to overcome fear before he could fully step into his calling. Timothy was from the city of Lystra in Asia Minor, born to a Jewish mother who became a Christian and a Greek father. Timothy was said to have been familiar with the Scriptures since childhood.

The Apostle Paul met him during his second missionary journey to Lystra. When Paul and Barnabas first visited Lystra, Paul healed a person crippled from birth, leading many of the people who lived there to believe in Jesus. When he returned a few years later with Silas, Timothy was already a respected member of the church, as were his grandmother Lois and his mother Eunice, both Jews.

Timothy became Paul's companion and co-worker. Paul thought of Timothy as a son, and he mentored him. Paul entrusted him with important assignments, and he wrote him at least two letters known as the First and Second Epistles to Timothy.

Just like many people in the church today, trusted elders and leaders spoke prophetic words over Timothy to confirm his calling and the plans God had for him. However, 1 Corinthians 16:10 implies that he was by nature shy and timid: *"When Timothy comes, see that you put him at ease among you, for he is doing the work of the Lord."*

Even though Timothy had genuine faith and a call of God on his life, he faced many of the same fears about being capable of fulfilling his calling that men and women face today. Paul included encouragement and instructions to help Timothy overcome the internal and external issues that he faced in both letters.

In his letters, Paul instructed Timothy to continue in prayer for all men, to set people in their proper place, to take heed to his ministry so he would not fall away, to give honor where it's due. To stay away from error and greed and instead pursue righteousness. To be unashamed of the gospel. To be loyal to the faith, to be strong in grace, and to approve and disapprove workers in the ministry. To be careful of perilous times and perilous men. To follow Paul's doctrine so he would not misrepresent the faith. To preach the word in season and out of season — whether people wanted to hear it or not, whether it was popular or not. (Read 1 and 2 Timothy)

Overseeing the church with all Paul's instructions was a huge mission. Paul knew Timothy would face times when he felt unsure of himself and his calling amidst the warfare that people whom God calls to leadership often do, so Paul took extra care to encourage Timothy to stand up to his fears, overcome them, and do the work of the ministry.

In Paul's first letter to Timothy, he wrote,

> *"This charge I entrust to you, Timothy, my child, in accordance with the prophecies previously made about you, that by them you may wage the good warfare," (1:18).*

In Paul's second letter to Timothy, he reminded him, *"God has not given us a spirit of fear, but of power and of love and of a sound mind" (1:6-8).*

The word *war* in 1 Timothy 1:18 means to execute God's divine will and to contend with carnal thoughts and feelings as a soldier in battle would against an enemy. We are not supposed to lie down and let our fears and insecurities overtake us. We are to contend for our prophecies: God's plans and promises that were spoken over us.

> *2 Corinthians 10:4–5 which I quoted in the chapter on mindsets, says, The weapons of our warfare are not carnal but mighty in God for pulling down strongholds, casting down arguments and every high thing that exalts itself*

against the knowledge of God, bringing every thought into captivity to the obedience of Christ.

This kind of warfare is done in prayer, where the power of God's word gives us the courage and inner strength to continue to fight and win our spiritual battles.

Paul knew that if Timothy believed he had the spirit of love, power, and a sound mind working in him and if focused on the prophetic words that were spoken over him he could overcome the self-doubt, fear, and anxiety he often felt. He knew the prophecies foretelling God's plans for him would be able to carry him through the difficult times and help him replace the lies that fought for space in his thoughts.

He knew that if Timothy would meditate on those prophetic words and believe what God said about him, he would have the courage to fight, to contend for, carry out, and execute his mission and fulfill his purpose.

Your calling statement is more than words on a piece of paper to puff you up and make you feel important. Let it stand as a written representation of all the prophetic words and the promises that were spoken over you.

The apostle Paul called the word of God the Sword of the Spirit. Use your calling statement and everything you wrote regarding your identity, your purpose, your mission, your vision, and your values as a weapon of war. In the book of Ephesians, Paul explains this war in more detail,

> *We do not wrestle against flesh and blood, but against principalities, against powers, against the rulers of the darkness of this age, against spiritual hosts of wickedness in the heavenly places. Therefore take up the whole armor of God, that you may be able to withstand in the evil day, and having done all, to stand. Stand therefore, having girded your waist with truth, having put on the breastplate of righteousness,*

and having shod your feet with the preparation of the gospel of peace; above all, taking the shield of faith with which you will be able to quench all the fiery darts of the wicked one. And take the helmet of salvation, and the sword of the Spirit, which is the word of God praying always with all prayer and supplication in the Spirit, being watchful to this end with all perseverance and supplication for all the saints—
(Ephesians 6:12-18)

Whatever God has called you to do, know that your flesh, the world, and your adversary, the devil will fight against you. Your flesh because it wants what it wants. The world because it does not love God, and some even hate God. The devil because he wants to render you ineffective. But take courage, Jesus has already triumphed over all things, and God will cause you to triumph through Him too if you continue to stand (Colossians 2:15 and 2 Corinthians 2:14).

CHAPTER 12

The Long Run

As I was writing this book, I began reading a book by Dave Ramsey, the *Money Makeover* and *Financial Peace University* guy. In the introduction, before I could even get into the book, I read the following words, "Years ago God called me to…"

Those words jumped out at me, and I had to put the book down for a moment to ponder on just what those few words meant coming from a man who is known for doing what God called him to do – help people get out of debt, stay out debt and thrive financially — God's way.

When I finished reading his story in the introduction of the book, the first thing that came to mind was the scripture verse *"the race is not to the swift" (Ecclesiastes 9:11).*

Dave Ramsey did not start in his calling where he is today. He started as a guy who found himself in debt and then learned how to get of debt and stay out, which then became the catalyst he needed to realize his calling to teach others what he implemented in his own life.

When he began walking in his calling, he self-published his first book and began selling it out of his car. He also started sharing his message on a local radio call-in show called The Money Game. That was a few decades ago.

As of the time I'm writing this book, Dave Ramsey is a best-selling author of six books on the New York Times, Wall Street Journal, and Publishers Weekly lists. He employs more than 550 people and has helped countless people reach their financial goals through a variety of products and services. His radio show is now nationally syndicated as *The Dave Ramsey Show*, and for the record, he is a Christian.

The Bible tells us, *"Though your beginning was small, yet your latter end would increase abundantly" (Job 8:7).* What started small became bigger than he could ask or imagine. I believe he was able to do all of these things because he was willing to run his race like a marathon. He was willing to stick with what God called him to do for the long run. His passion fueled his purpose because he believed in what he was called to do.

However, unlike Dave Ramsey, some people go after their calling like it's a sprint. They expect things to happen overnight. If things don't work out as fast or how they think they should, instead of pressing into their calling, they give up and pursue other things. But our God-given callings take time and perseverance.

When God calls you to do something, you have to be willing to commit to it for the long run. You have to be faithful in the little things before God entrusts you with greater things. You have to be in it not just for yourself but for the significance of the work you are called to do and the people you are called to reach, whether few or many.

In this age of social media, it's easy to want to give up when you think you're not moving forward in your calling, whatever that may be, at the same pace other people seem to be. However, looking at what other people are doing can cause you to get off track from accomplishing what God called you to do.

Reading Dave Ramsey's story reminded me of when God first called me and showed me my purpose and my mission. It reminded me of how far along I've come, and how far I still have to go. His story reminded me of just how important it is to do the daily work in front of me.

His story reminded me that it's good to dream big, but I also need to pace myself for the long run because a calling is like a marathon.

I was reminded to step out on faith in the things I know God called me to do but not to despise small beginnings. I was reminded to stay focused, knowing that if I stay in the race, I will make it to my expected end.

God's calling does not mean things will come effortlessly or quickly. Not everything you do will go as you hope or plan. You will have to step out on faith and sometimes make mistakes only to learn from those mistakes, get back up, and try again. You will have to work hard and grind for it. You will have to determine within yourself to be in it for the long run, do the daily work, and stay the course.

Take a moment before you continue to read to re-commit to your calling for the long run and to put measures in place to pace yourself so you won't get discouraged if things take longer than you think.

CHAPTER 13

Upward

The race God called us to is not only long, but it is a continuous lifestyle of upward movement, leaving the past behind and pressing on to know Him more.

The Apostle Paul said:

I do not count myself to have apprehended; but one thing I do, forgetting those things which are behind and reaching forward to those things which are ahead, I press toward the goal for the prize of the upward call of God in Christ Jesus. (Philippians 3:13-14)

This upward call is a call to the called: an invitation to those who have said yes to the call of God to continue heavenward, reaching for God, going deeper and higher with Him.

However, Paul warned that for "the called" of God to answer the high calling of God we must be willing to continue to forget what is behind us: the good works we've done as well as the sins we've committed, the mistakes we've made, and our accomplishments.

We must be willing to forgive the people who hurt us, and those who let us down or left us. And, if God should require it, we must be willing to let go of the people who loved us and were there for us along the way. We must be willing to let go of anything and anyone if need be for the privilege of knowing and following Jesus.

However, not everyone is willing or ready to pay the full price required for the high calling.

Jesus explained this way:

> *For which of you, intending to build a tower, does not sit down first and count the cost, whether he has enough to finish it — lest, after he has laid the foundation and is not able to finish, all who see it begin to mock him, saying, 'This man began to build and was not able to finish'? Or what king, going to make war against another king, does not sit down first and consider whether he is able with ten thousand to meet him who comes against him with twenty thousand? Or else, while the other is still a great way off, he sends a delegation and asks conditions of peace. So likewise, whoever of you does not forsake all that he has cannot be My disciple. (Luke 14:28-33)*

There is another gospel being preached that promises an easy road and assures you that you won't have to give up anything at all, that God will come alongside you and bless whatever you choose to do. I assure you, if you answer yes to the upward call, you will find this other gospel isn't true.

Rarely will God's plans for you line up with what you had in mind for your life before saying yes to God. You have to be willing to lose your life and give up the life you planned to gain the life God planned for you.

Submitting your plans to God can be difficult when He asks for something you do not want to let go. However, whenever God asks you for something, it's because He has something better planned for you.

If you learn to trust God even when you don't understand Him and to rely on the truth — that He knows what best for you because He created you and He knows His plans for you, surrendering your plans will not be so hard to do.

Unfortunately, many people decide at some point in their upward journey that the cost is too high to continue following Christ. They want what they want more than they want to fulfill God's purpose and plans, so they turn back and lose their way. Many lose their eternal reward, as well. But God has not called you to draw back but to continue to press toward the goal so you can receive what He has promised you – a crown of righteousness given only to those who finish their race, (2 Timothy 4:8).

CHAPTER 14

Choose What Matters

In the story of Mary and Martha, the two sisters that became friends with Jesus, we see two very different lifestyles:

> *Now it happened as they went that He entered a certain village, and a certain woman named Martha welcomed Him into her house. And she had a sister called Mary, who also sat at Jesus' feet and heard His word. But Martha was distracted with much serving, and she approached Him and said, 'Lord, do You not care that my sister has left me to serve alone? Therefore tell her to help me.' And Jesus answered and said to her, 'Martha, Martha, you*

are worried and troubled about many things. But one thing is needed, and Mary has chosen that good portion, which will not be taken away from her.' (Luke 10:37–42)

Mary chose to make sitting at Jesus' feet her highest priority while Martha was what I like to call a serve-oholic. She was So distracted by serving other people that she neglected the most important person — Jesus — spending time with Him at His feet, hearing His words.

The Bible defines being *distracted* as having care, worry, or anxiousness. It comes from a root word that means to part, share, to disunite, distribute, divide, or give in part.

Many women live distracted lifestyles. Like Martha, their attention is divided among too many things. They are worried and concerned about so many things that they forget to make time for the things that matter.

They often neglect time with God (intimate fellowship, not just reading and prayer out of a sense of religious duty) and the things God has called them to do for the seemingly urgent things. They thrive on busyness, activity, and creative energy — what some would call healthy chaos.

Others are "yes" people who haven't learned how to say no without feeling guilty or like they aren't doing their part in whatever they've gotten themselves involved in whether or not God told them to. If they get asked to join a group, donate their time, be on a committee, or part of a ministry, they say yes without considering the cost to them, their families, and the other the things that really matter to them.

However, saying yes to everyone else will leave you overwhelmed with more work than you realize you signed up for and without enough time and energy to focus on what God called you to do. I know this to be true because, for a long time, like Martha, I was a serve-oholic. And, if I'm not careful, I can slip back into that mode very easily.

I'm a creative person, so I have to stop myself from venturing into new projects. At one time, I was a yes person until I learned how to say no and walk away without making excuses or feeling like I have to give a satisfactory explanation to the other person or parties involved.

Trying to do it all left me with little spiritual and physical strength or time to focus on cultivating my relationship with Jesus and being a good steward of the life and relationships He had already given me. This kind of busyness is not God's plan for His children.

Busyness is one of the devil's great strategies against Christians. He wants us to believe that our good works can replace the time that we should spend with the Lord. He knows that time spent with Jesus is the one thing that without question has eternal value.

When my children were young and I was going through my divorce, I went back to school to finish my degree. I also started working fulltime. Not because I had to, but because I felt like I had something to prove. I had lost my identity as being a wife, and I thought that a degree and a career would give me back my sense of self-worth. I went from being a stay-at-home mom to having a new busy life and trying to balance it all with being a mom to four kids still in elementary school and very busy schedules of their own.

My distracted lifestyle led to physical and emotional burnout, which led to spiritual apathy. One night in the middle of trying to do it all, I don't remember when but fell asleep on the couch. I woke up with the TV blaring, food still on the table, and my kids sound asleep in their beds. They had put themselves to bed but left the cleaning for me.

I knew then that some things had to go. I decided to live more intentionally by rearranging my life around the people and things that matter to me and the things God called me to do.

During this process, I had to admit that a lot of what I was doing wasn't necessary for me to be who God called me to be or do what He called me to do. So I learned to say no and how to let go of things that God never called me to do.

When I began focusing on what matters, my lifestyle changed. A lifestyle is how a person spends their time and their way of life, including patterns of behavior, interactions, what they consume, their work, activities, and interests.

Spending time with Jesus became the best most important part of my day. I became more intentional. I was able to be fully present for the people I love, and I had time to do what God called me to do.

The truth is, we all get to choose our lifestyles and what we will give our time and attention. We can be like Martha —so worried and distracted by the "many things" that we forget to focus on the few important things. Or we can be like Mary and choose to prioritize the things that matter above the seemingly urgent and distracting things.

To choose what matters is to put God and the things that He's called you to do first and invest your time and energy in the people and things that are important to you. To choose what matters is to be committed enough to your God-given calling to consistently focus on your God-given goals, but also be surrendered enough to the Holy Spirit to recognize His leading and be willing to turn aside from your daily routine if He leads you in a different direction.

It doesn't mean you don't serve others. It means you count the cost of saying yes and how your yes will take away from the roles and responsibilities you've already committed to doing and the things God called you to do. It means inquiring of God before you commit to new things.

Unfortunately, it also means that sometimes you will disappoint people. But disappointing people is always better than disappointing God.

Your Daily Dare

In his letter to the church of Rome, the apostle Paul encouraged believers to devote themselves to their gifts and callings as a sign of appreciation for God's kindness in giving such wonderful gifts freely,

> God in his kindness gave each of us different gifts. If your gift is prophesying, prophesy. If your gift is serving, then devote yourself to serving. If it is teaching, devote yourself to teaching. If it is encouraging others, devote yourself to giving encouragement. If it is sharing, be generous. If it is leadership, lead enthusiastically. If it is helping people in need, help them cheerfully. (Romans 12:6-8 God's Word)

Paul wasn't saying that believers should focus all of our time and energy on our gifts, and nothing else. He was trying to express that we should be devoted to our callings, and make time for what God called us to do by prioritizing what He says is important.

I dare you to devote time to sitting with Jesus every morning to hear His words, to intentionally declaring your calling statement, and also set aside time to give attention using your gifts for the things God has called you to do. Choosing to do these three things each day will create consistent clarity and help you live intentionally.

On the next page, using smart goals, create a plan for how you can implement these three disciplines into your daily routine.

S.M.A.R.T. goals are

Specific – they state exactly what you will focus on and what you want to accomplish.

Measurable – they state how you will accomplish your goals, and how will you know each goal has been accomplished?

Achievable – they are doable for you. Stretch yourself, and don't be afraid to grow, but don't take on more than you called to do.

Relevant – they help you accomplish your vision and mission, and they are in line with your calling and your purpose.

Time-bound –they have set a time to be completed.

Krista Pettiford